B
Ψ

BuddyLitZine.com

Buddy. a lit zine.
Issue #3 (10/18)

MASTHEAD
Founding/Chief Editor
David Welper

Editors/Readers
Fiction
Sierra Crumbaker
Selina Scheumann

Poetry
Adam Crittenden
Taylor Gianfrancisco
Maura Monaghan
Ashley Steineger

Non-Fiction
Lizzy Burnam
Hannah Redigan

Event & Zine Layout Assistance
Sierra Crumbaker

Liaisons/Consultants
J deSalvo
Dena Igusti
Jesse Scott Owen
Laurel Shimasaki
Autumn Slaughter

Cover: *Süßigkeiten* by Mark Brasuell

CONTENTS

LETTER FROM THE EDITOR

This issue marks our first year of existence. While it's always tough to get something going, it's also exciting to see it develop. In the past year, we've added some editors and liaisons to help out. Thanks to the *Buddy* team for your help.

To celebrate our first year, *Buddy* is hosting our very first ever reading event at Innisfree Poetry Bookstore in Boulder, CO on October 9th, 2018. The event is also a book drive for mental health patients and consumers. Thanks to Dennis, ari, Simone, and Evan for being featured readers. Thanks to Innisfree for the venue. Thanks to Brooklyn Arts Press for donating your books to *Buddy*.

Buddy is switching gears a bit. We will start accepting writing on any topic but will remain a safe space for writing about mental health. We will continue to support mental health issues and communities.

Remember to take care of yourself. Take a bit of time to relax, do something fun. Put your cell phone away, meet up with a friend for coffee once in a while. Read a book or lit zine from an indie/small press. And keep writing!

David Welper, RN, BSN, BS, MA
Founder/EIC
www.BuddyLitZine.com

"Süßigkeiten" (Acrylic on canvas, 2018) Mark Brasuell

THE RUNAWAY

Sean Ireland

So, we chased him into the dark basement and backed him up into a corner. His face was white as alabaster. He glowed. I held the rock tightly in my hand. I told him to hand the pocketbook over. He did. It was empty. Where were the food stamps? Where was the bracelet? Gone, he said. He had to eat. I stared at him for a moment. He was thin, like a blade of white milkweed. His teeth were yellow. He was wearing a ragged checkered shirt and blue pants that didn't fit him any longer. He said he was sorry that he'd stolen it but that he hadn't eaten in three days. I didn't believe him. That was impossible. What did he do? Slept, he said, and roamed the streets all night long looking for something to steal, something he could sell. He hadn't found anything, so he came back to our house at dawn. The front door was open, as it always was. My mother's pocketbook was on the kitchen table. He'd grabbed it and fled.

He was someone I'd helped hide. I'd hid him in our basement until it became too dangerous. It was cold and he would wait for Billy and I to bring him a sandwich or something to drink. I would come down in the morning and he'd be in a corner on the cold and dusty concrete floor covered in dirty laundry. He slept with his knees to his chest. He didn't go to school. He roamed the city, sat on benches, sat in parks, slept in the afternoons in empty pavilions and on the back porches of the old ladies in the neighborhood. He had no one. He had no family. He had nobody to stand up for him. And when they came for him, the foster people, they came in a posse with belts and ropes and they tied him often by his ankles and dragged him home. Once we hid him in a garage loft but someone, one of the kids in the neighborhood, found out and told his family. They encircled the garage. He tried to jump out the back window, but they caught him, broken and exhausted, in a woodpile. They hog tied him and carried him home. He was sweating and his shirt was nearly off him and he was crying and kicking so wildly that a man stopped and got out of his car and questioned the woman, the foster mom. I thought he was gonna take Kenneth home, be his father. Instead, he got into his car and left. Kenneth didn't want to go back to the foster home. They took him in only for the money, he said. They beat him and kept him in a small room on the third floor. They didn't feed him. I believed him, especially because he was always ravenous and always skinny.

I yanked the pocketbook from his hand, gripped the rock tightly. I looked into the pocketbook. It was empty and black and smelled like my mother's perfume. I felt through the Kleenex and found the cigarette lighter, smooth in my hand. He edged back into the darkness and the cold. I was holding the pocketbook in one hand, light as a feather, filthy from his carrying it with him for three days, and the sharp rock in the other. He backed up against the wall, his chest rising up and down rapidly. He'd been beaten so often and chased so much and cornered and slammed to the ground and tied up by belts and whipped that I was surprised he was still sensitive to it. I was really mad that he'd taken my mom's pocketbook but, in that moment, looking at him standing there against the darkened wall of the basement, I felt that familiar wave of compassion. I let the rock down and I asked him if he'd eaten that morning. He said no. He'd spent my mother's money two days before on slices of pizza and soda and a bag of sliced white bread and peanut butter and marshmallow. I handed the rock to Billy, told Kenneth I didn't want him around the house anymore. I didn't know what else to say. I wasn't interested in saving anyone, and yet I'd been hiding him, helping him to run away, so I guess to some extent I was. I wanted him to have a better life and I didn't understand why he didn't have a family and it wasn't making any sense to me.

The three of us came out of the basement beneath the Belmont Avenue Apartments and went into the Cumberland Farms on the first floor. The woman behind the counter said she didn't want him in the store. He'd stolen candy and chocolate milk. She threatened to call the police. Kenneth walked out immediately and crossed the street and sat down on a curb while Billy and I bought what we could, once again, what we thought might sustain him for the night—Yodels, State Line Potato Chips, A Coke, two graham patties filled with cream. We carried it across the street in a paper bag and handed it to him. He opened it, reached in, started eating the Yodels right away. I watched him closely as he stuffed one of the cakes in his mouth and washed it down with Coke. He burped, looked around. I noticed a scar above his left eye. He started to cry. He cried a lot. Billy and I sat down and waited. The sun was setting and it was getting cold. He asked me again if he could come to the house, sleep in the basement. He promised he would never steal my mother's pocketbook again. I couldn't do it. They were all looking for him. I had to tell my mother that we'd kept him in the basement a few nights before and that he was the one who'd probably stolen the pocketbook and now it was confirmed. I was bringing it home, empty and scuffed up. He'd been carrying the thing around with him for three days. Why didn't he just throw it away?

The streetlight above us suddenly turned on. We looked up. The sky was leaden grey. The electric light was dim at first and then began to glow and buzz. A truck rumbled by. A blackbird landed in the middle of the street and started pecking at something solid and very dead. He started crying again. We stood up, muttered something about seeing him the next day. He said he wished he would die. I told him he shouldn't think that way. I wanted somebody to stop right then and there, a man, someone who would take him into a good home. I wanted the grownups to take responsibility for him—for this—for us. I wanted someone to save him and there was nobody there to save him but us and we couldn't do it anymore. Billy had to go. His grandfather was making pizza and he had to be home by six. We cut through the lot and started down Garfield Street. I looked back at him as we walked. He was eating the last of the cream cakes. He had the frosting all over his mouth.

AS EVERY MORNING OF ALL THE MORNINGS IN THE WORLD
Rachele Salvini

The buzz of the TV at 5 in the morning does not wake her up. She lies on the sofa, her left arm hanging over. The white light of dawn spills on her face like milk, but she does not open her eyes. She's cold. The red fleece blanket is on the floor.
Curled on it, he snores. Soft breaths in the silence.
She hears the TV speaker but does not listen.
This female orangutan is 42 years old and has been taking care of her cub for six.

The tiles of the floor are cold and pale, scattered with crumpled handkerchiefs like clouds on the winter sea. Between them, the vet's number, scribbled on a yellow post. She feels his humid nose brushing against her fingers. She thinks she's dreaming.
Maybe she's getting used to his absence.
He may not be there in a few hours.
The orangutan is the primate that takes care of their cubs the longest, after us.

The claws click on the ceramic: coffee grains poured into a small cup. She hears him moving around the room with difficulty. He's slow. It's not a dream. He walks around the place as he usually does when dawn turns into morning.
David Attenborough's voice tells her about faraway lands. On the Ethiopian planes the sun is rising, as it is happening now in her living room.
As every day that begins.
As every morning of all the mornings in the world.

She feels his wet nose against her fingers again, to wake her up. She needs to get up, fumble for her glasses, grab the tartan leash that hangs from the heater and go out in the biting cold.
As every morning of all the mornings in the world.

***

Everything has gone as it should.
He's gone.

The stars begin to crackle in the black sky. She lies on the sofa again. The handkerchiefs are still there, right beside the post with the vet's number. Tonight there is a Coke can and an empty box of chicken nuggets. She wraps herself up with the red fleece blanket.

After mating for her first time, the female octopus looks for a good place to lay her eggs. This will be her home for six months, during which she won't eat anything: she will be too busy protecting her future offspring. It's dark. Her hand slips towards the floor, and her fingertips sense the cold ceramic again. The next day is already coming. The sun will rise in a while. As every morning of all the mornings in the world.

When the eggs start to hatch, the female octopus is dying. This mother accomplishes the greatest act of love: in order to protect her offspring, she starves herself to death, sacrificing herself for the life that will come.

The red fleece blanket is warm. She thinks this is a good way to end the day, to finally close the eyes for the last time. It is scattered with blonde hairs, but she does not care. The tartan leash hangs over the heater as every day.

She watches the microscopic octopuses slipping out of their eggs. New life, minuscule hearts bumping in the ocean for the first time. She feels them swimming between the fingers of her hand. She looks at the mother's corpse pirouetting away in the current and inhales the smell of the red fleece blanket. Again.

The tiny octopuses twirled and played around her fingertips, dampening her hands. As if, despite everything, she is not really alone.

It's Sunday morning. She ties her hair up, crushes the Coke can, the chicken nuggets empty box, the handkerchiefs and the post with the vet's number. She puts everything into a big sack.

She folds the red fleece blanket carefully. She is not sure if she wants to wash it. She decides she can wait. Then she drinks a cup of coffee at the window, the winter sun burning her cheeks.

She does not go out this morning.

The tartan leash keeps on hanging over the heater of the living room, all Sunday and then everyday of her life. When she looks at it, she feels life, strong and powerful as never before, hitting her like dawn lights in the morning.

When she looks at the leash, the intensity of life reveals itself in all its glory, as a red fleece blanket scattered with blonde hair. As claws that clicked on the floor to come wake her up.

When she looks at the leash, she feels many tiny octopuses spinning around her fingers, just like a nose trying to catch her attention as she slept, just like life going on after the end. As an octopus mother that sailed the ocean, forever.

"Rainy Day in Boulder" Jacob Newman

ARTICULATIONS BETWEEN THINGS SAID

Jason Dean Arnold

Every electrical device in our home needs to be checked

Again   checked
Again   checked
Again   checked
Again.

The light switch doesn't know that it can't be controlled
With my mind; I stare at it, examine
                              Its resting position.

When I was a child, I would close my eyes to hold the image
As a temporary imprint on the insides of my eyelids.

It would quickly devolve into pentimento, trace, fleshy abstract,
Erasure.

The beauty is in the longing, the lost.
I am losing everything everyday, in small moments, repeated

Again.

Again.

I only trust the failure of my memory.

FIFTYSIXHOURS
Robert Beveridge

fifty-six hours. hands on clocks and fallen
madonnas. time expands, contracts, moves
on. fifty-six hours. sleep, write, try on
the new cassock with the split pocket
and see if it looks good with your favorite
black skirt. loose and soft, rubs
against you. you touch yourself
beneath it in front of the two-way mirror.
fifty-six hours. you will wear it
and he will touch you.

time has no fingers, only hands. they slap.
the robot side of you works while free
in your mind you are in the ladies' room
of the bar with him inside you, his eyes
on yours, whispers of love.
fifty-six hours. you can smell cigarette
smoke and sex on the crotch
of your pants. wear it well. fifty-six
hours. change clothes again
and wait for time's contraction.

BELIEVE IT OR NOT
John M. Davis

he said rooms didn't spin
very often. walls just came alive
with ants and rats.
sometimes birds
flew out of the wallpaper.
thick black mud might exude
up through the floor, as if by sieve
cap to a giant extrusion machine
hydraulics unseen.
When he needed to rouse his demons
or drown them, he went to Brad's Bar
the only bar on earth
that covered a full city block
believe it or not
on the shortest street in the world –
Judd Place, Oakland, California –
which is where he'd leave me
six, seven years old, sitting in a car.

TO MY BOYFRIEND, WHOSE FAMILY KEEPS ME AROUND
Breia Gore

I am trying to love your family in a tangent way,
without thinking of calloused palms or eating bones.
In their eyes, New York City and summer vacation mean the same thing,
in their eyes bad grades and praying both mean rebellions.
I do not need to be strung along like stars or a conspiracy-theorist board,
knotted into your flesh like a wedding veil or your mothers knitting
needle.
I do not need to be taken in but your mouth is kind. You are all so kind,
more of me
and your house will overflow.
You can't take any more boxes of me throwing up in your bathroom.
Without you, nobody would pick me up for rolled ice cream or see me
cry
on new years eve. Who I am transitions into "his family invited me" and
I am always trying to keep the invitation.
And when I think I can do it all on my own I see the uproar of the
railroad
 pulling into the station at three in the morning. My unbrushed teeth,
my sleepy feet tripping down the stairs, I hear every passenger's jealousy.
Having the weight of your sibling's footsteps memorized is as honest as I
can be.

SURREALISTIC CIRCUS
Lindsey Morrison Grant

It is where I move along to the gallery of same-sex sandwiches
     Corridors of condiments and condemnation that entreat me and
     repeat
     Revulsions that make my eyes water from within and without

It is where I move along to the bemusement of the moneychangers
     With oily-pompadours and scaly smiles who seduce virginal
     buds of solitary joy
     With Kewpie dolls that weep from within and without

It is where I move along to the carnival of barren billets,
     Respite from wanton favors and rhyme. It speaks of the daze of
     summer
     Which make my heart break from within and without

It is where I glide along the midway of freaks and pinheads
     The zealot whispers the walrus song; the barker offers me one on
     a stick
     In the lad of screams, I must choose from within or without

It is where I am. I am trying to move along, my head a Casaba
     My feet a blacksmith's envy. The stale corridors, sterile hopes
     and baby soaps
     The observed, observer and absurd, to my chagrin and my doubt

HUNTER-GATHERER
Debbie Hall

> *It takes a courageous/person to leave spaces/empty.*
> — Kay Ryan

Daily she feeds found objects
to her house--
dented hubcaps,
cases of empty Coke
bottles, stuffed
bears missing
their glass eyes,
hundreds of plastic bags,
gently used.
Old
National Geographics
stacked in columns
form a labyrinth
of narrow passages,
air spaces shrinking
like aging lungs.
After each night's rest,
she resumes
her dogged pursuit
of the disappearing edge
of enough.

COMPOST
Dustin Stephens

I can't
remember

how you
used to
peel oranges

did I
have to help

or did you
shred their skin
to confetti

or was it
all in one go
leaving a
spiral and nine
slices of veined
juice

TUCKERMANNOPSIS CHLOROPHYLLA
Dennis James Sweeney

The summer waved its bones
Lightning shrank
Lively Chorus 1
The clouds a payment
Shoes lost to the bubbling night
Our shrouds
Lively Chorus 2
Catch on shells
3, 4, 5
We want ice cold until we venture in

GYMNOSTOMUM RECURVIROSTRUM
Dennis James Sweeney

We won the meat prize
Sunday was God's
Less is less than more
But it does its best
The hills sing in the trees
The hills
We try desperately to contain ourselves

BUXBAUMIA PIPERI
Dennis James Sweeney

Cars chase themselves
A bucket of white paint simmers
After so many burials
We know what we are looking for
And where
And thanklessly

HAUNTED STILL-LIFE GALLERY
Anastasia Jill

Loving every single vein in your body
I ghost their blue bodies
with fingertips,

complaining against understanding skin
I can't feel close enough

I'm thankful for spirits
joint bones like headstones,
my galleria, coffins are for flowers -

who says the grave
can't spur growth?

MOXIE
Anastasia Jill

I'd die for you,
and it's quite alright.

I have strength,
somewhere in you,
in your gameless
green aura.

IN THE KITCHEN
Jonathan May

I wake up feeling the tightness behind my eyes
which means I had the dream where you were on fire.
I couldn't do anything to stop it (tied hands, bodies,

      all the bodies filled with salt)

I couldn't even cut myself open and stuff you inside
where my warm mucous cave could choke out
the flames of your paperhands, laced with ink

(the delicious taste of ink) and the green dress you wore
with your hairy legs poking from beneath, turning trans-
-lucent at the calves. *Mr. Cactus Legs, take me dancing*

                      tonight

And all morning—as I make rye toast and try to fold the egg
white over the yolk (the pocket of heat, the surprise, the gush
                    of sunshine)—
I catch myself dancing in the kitchen,
just a two-step here   and a two-step there,
my mouth aswill with grape juice,
and you—your vanished knees.

This is my blood, don't cry now, just drink it.

Just turn there in the green dress, and let me spit juice
all over you until you are nothing but ash.

Later, as I sweep up the broken plates, mop up
the egg yolk, I don't know what to do with what's left
of you, the translucence.

NYCTOPHILIAC
Mia Herman

Because the air smells different
when the light falls back

and the whoosh of the wind
after crawling into bed

and the percussion of cicadas
is an update on weather

and the roads begin breathing
when the speed limit wears off

and the creak of the floorboards
as the house winds down

and the right words come faster
when nobody says anything

ECHOES
Mia Herman

"Empathy is about finding echoes of another person in yourself"
— Mohsin Hamid

But what if I don't want to find your echoes
inside of me, bouncing off bones
and sinking into belly fat,
wreaking havoc on my body
from the inside out?

What if all I want is to uproot you,
cut you out completely
until I am missing
lips and limbs
and organs
and all my vital signs
are flat-lining
and I am finally back
to life?

ON THE BOUND TO YOUR LOVE
Simone Liggins

If I say to you the owls aren't what they seem,
you'll know that comes from someone else's dream.

With bloody blows, we battle verses
and the rights to wield them on tongues like curses.

Oh say, this is what I see:
We the people aren't truly free.

By the by, I can't really lie;
call me an afflicted Gemini.
.
Weaving words craft fresh spells,
but for what I want, only a few I'll tell.

Hold tight, count down from nine—
this is how you read the spirals of time.

I work it wild, a hurricane heart is true.
For one sweet-centered eye, I spin this for you.

ME TOO
ari lips

that day
i wore the blazer
the pants
and the shoes i bought
 for the case i had to testify
 in earlier that year
the shoes a knock-off version of the kind
my attorney then wore
because she was so effortlessly poised and professional
and i wanted to be that, or something like it
so i wore them again for my deposition
i took my piercings out
did my makeup perfect
subtle, conservative
piled my braids on top of my head
with every bobby pin i've ever owned
painted my nails fresh blood red,
because that's what i do
when i need to be a giant
and i certainly looked the part
even if i couldn't find my motivation
i knew they would be asking for it
and i still hadn't come up with anything
because what they were really looking for
would be an explanation
and i didn't have one
i still don't
but i looked like i knew what i was doing
so, i drove to my attorney's office
they asked me to come early
so i got there before then
and their secretary got me water
and she sat me down at
the head of a big, empty mahogany table
and i left the perfect red lip-print on the glass
as i watched the video they told me to watch
on how to give a good deposition,
which is basically don't lie,

but don't tell them anything
if they're not asking for it
but i'd done this before
so i wondered to myself about the actors instead
things like: was this their crowning achievement
and how many takes did they do
of the woman losing her composure over seemingly nothing?
and why weren't any of them black?
begging to be distracted, or even better
dismissed,
but then it was over and it was time
and my attorney sat me down at another
big, mahogany table, not empty
but not full
and we sat; the opposing counsel,
my counsel,
myself,
and a stenographer.
i took an oath
knowing they'd be asking for it
but i still didn't-
opposing counsel proceeded to ask me
unrelated questions to later
prove whether or not i'm a liar
who is my family
where did i work in college
what did i eat for lunch the day of my accident
then he'd hand me medical documents
and i'd tell him
what i knew about the medical documents
which wasn't much, honest
and i'd promised myself i would keep it together
but i'd also known it was coming,
he's going to be asking for it
but i'd pretend that i didn't know, hard
and i'd fool even myself until:
"deposition exhibit 5 was marked
question by Mr. Coberly: Ms. Lipscomb I've handed you what's marked
as exhibit 5
(i read the date and i already know)
Answer:...uh huh
Q: do you recognize this at all?

A:No.
(because they don't show you the patient report when you're the-)
Q: we received this in response to a waiver you signed
(pt was found face down and unresponsive on the pavement)
Answer: Oh. Right…
(pt became combative when approached by staff)
Q: and it relates to an emergency room visit in 2013. Do you see that?
A: Yes.
(pt became combative when approached by staff)
(oh, that's why they restrained me)
Q: What is this in relation to?"
and i told them.
i told all of them.
the stenographer didn't document
the tears that erupted from somewhere
deep inside my repressed trauma
so suddenly, volcanic
 i didn't even notice they were there
but i never let them fall anyway
and she didn't note
how my body was doing that thing
where it wants to be sobbing
but i won't let it so it's
just gasping for air in defiance
she just wrote that they asked if i needed to take a break
which is a really compassionate way to say
"get it the fuck together"
and i go to the bathroom
and i stare at the window
looking for a place where it's okay to scream now
and the tears can fall without ruining my makeup
but it's stained glass, so i can't see a way out
 see, i'd never told anyone about that night
including myself
i told people my teeth were
broken because i slipped on ice
and nothing else
because i didn't know anything else
all i know is i woke up in a hospital
strapped to a bed; naked
 staff assumed i was just a
 too-drunk angry, black girl

37

and made me use a bedpan instead of
taking the restraints off because
i guess i was more fight than flight that day
or maybe i was a lot of both
and i didn't correct anyone
because i couldn't admit what happened
i just let them think
what they already wanted to think
what they always think
i was a too drunk, too angry, too black
 girl that needed to learn her lesson
because she couldn't just keep it the fuck together-
but i promised i would so
a long 60 seconds letter
i sat back down at the table
and i don't remember answering
any other questions
but i know that i did, because i
 got the transcript in the mail today.
and i don't remember leaving; driving home
but i know that i did, because
when i got to my house i was
still in the driver seat
and i don't remember going inside,
to my room, sitting down
 on the floor and finally letting the tears fall wherever
but i know that I did because
there was mascara all over my blazer
and i don't remember
taking off my knock-off shoes
 but i know that I did
 because i remember laughing, maniacal
in that maudlin-sideshow-bob way
that doesn't come from anywhere truly humorous
 because of all the days i've worn these stupid shoes
without ever reading what the label said
out of every time i wore them
and played pretend professional
for the past year almost
without noticing the label
today would be the fucking day.
me too.

I'LL CREATE
Evan James Sheldon

I'll create
a mythology
of self. I'll be
dragon. I'll be
goblin. I'll be
rock. I'll be
fortress
wide & offering
succor. I'll be
dark side
of the moon—
perhaps defender,
back turned
to this light,
face blazing
beneath a million
others. I'll be
good pastor,
calm pasture,
gaping chasm. I'll be
all this and nothing
more. I am
growing
soon to be
brimming
with newness.

from RKVRY [3+++]
Gerard Sarnat

2...Alzhie's...

"Old age isn't a
battle:
old age is a
massacre."
-- Philip Roth,
Everyman

On that babbling
Mon-
day morning...
despite
Nintendo
brain training...
old enough
you're
not premature...

under attack
damn
plaquetangles...
I've wandered
away
into the past...
can't find
unlockers
or my seers...
which they say's
ok
but a problem...
when I put
glasses
in the door...
or try to use
keys
to help read...

once I was an
MD
who knew...
what ApoE 4
genes
prophesied...
there was an
enzyme
name escapes
me...
to snip in an
apoE2
like fertilizer...
Mediterranean
diet

lots of sleep...
kids feed me
turmeric
...cotton balls...

those good old
days
gone in ether...
slipsliding
thudthud
devolution...
densely sedated
lizard
at times
vacant...
now mostly
wild-eyed
and blue-
lipped...
with a little
pooling of
pond scum
spittle...

as a west coast
smart
aleck at
Harvard...
I spent
Thanksgivings
nearby
Lincoln...
turned out not
far from
Thoreau's
Walden...
with Walter
Cannon
a classmate...
plus his gracious
family
they took me
in...
handgliding
down from
Cannon Hill....
named for
Walter Sr.
icon coined...
the term
homeostasis
my bodymind...
may have lost
forever –
no recovery.

"Voices" Sonia Fierce

LAST OF THE DINOSAURS
Anna Kaye-Rogers

Everyone has a story of the time I almost died, and almost no one remembers the same time. I am found on floors, hidden in closets, lurking next to beds and huddled into strange corners. I am ten feet behind and fading fast, pitifully clutching at purses and backpacks for an inhaler. I am stuck at the foot of the stairs, pressed against the seat of the car, feet pushed hard against the floorboards, panting. I slam the bedroom door shut when I want to sit out at the bonfire. I pull the sleeve of my hoodie over my nose, nails digging into my cheek. I will not allow the smoke inhalation to kill me when I could just as easily suffocate myself. I am broken inside, unable to function and incapable of saving myself. I gasp for air greedily, and it is never enough. Which instability came first, mental or physical?

There are stages to my impending doom, years spent minimizing and rationalizing, lying to myself until the truth is a newfound discovery. I am always surprised to be dying and always surprised to still be alive. There is a lack of oxygen, lack of blood, lack of brain waves, and yet I am always surprised for the lack of good judgment shown when I most need it. I resist the call to my inhaler; I want to fight it and break it, control it and overpower it, but the thing I am fighting is me. I resist living as much as dying, one ragged breath away from never coming back and one good breath away from being fine again. I hesitate. I wait. I have never once wheezed myself back to quiet breaths, never forced my chest to expand to an easy, peaceful night of sleep. Yet still I try, never long enough to die but longer than I should if I deserved to live. I am an evolutionary flaw, a Darwinian easy target, meant for biological death and human cannon fodder. I am genetically weak, biologically imperfect. My fight or flight instinct is as broken as my lungs. Scientifically I don't deserve to live, unable to shake a canister and administer my own life-saving treatment. It hurts so bad to breathe tears form. My vocal chords make sounds without me, echoes of animal pain my species no longer speaks. It is a high-pitched wheeze with a low, shallow growl, the two directions I could have evolved in perfect unstable harmony, and yet the inhaler stays unused in my hand. Fighting makes it worse, makes it hurt, leaves me with headaches and chest aches and back aches and shoulder aches for days. My body begs for oxygen, but it has no air to speak. I have refused to give it what it needs most, because it refuses to let me have it. I would rather die than take one more breath. Breathing should be easy. Whole sayings are based on the principle. Yet for me even the simplest of takes, the most basic, are beyond my capability. I am as fucking useless as my lungs. My stubbornness was meant to keep me alive until I can release a burst of medicated air, but it keeps me from inhaling.

There's a certain smugness in my trips to the ER, a sense of validation from the hospital bracelet that scuffs incessantly at my wrist. I am too skinny for comfort, my own bones turning against me and protruding into my personal space. The purple veins down my arm are angrily close to the surface, written in thick sharpie markers when I wanted thin pen lines. I am pale and the hospital gown is too loose, tied as tightly as it can. I fear sometimes I'm the last of the dinosaurs, the vertebrae of my back too obvious to be anything than spikes. But I need the assurance that it's bad enough to warrant a trip here, need to confirm that asthma is dangerous and someday it will kill me. I need to know that the feeling of never getting enough air as I drown without a drop of water; need to understand that the greedy fingers choking off my air supply are strangling me from the inside out. I am my own worst enemy. Knowing I am at a war, a real war, with stakes and consequences and death when I am unable to confront my own mortality and still make it to my classes, I suffocate under the pressure. I believe it is real and so I make it worse, because the anxiety of not breathing makes the not breathing worse, and then I am anxious. The symptoms of a panic attack and an asthma attack are almost identical. I cannot tell the difference between them, which is the trigger and which is the intensifier. By the time I remember that my symptoms are real and my fears are legitimate, it does not matter. I am past the point of return. Only my inhaler can save me now. And I am too disgusted with myself for reaching this point to use it. I feel I have to earn my life, have to suffer first in order to learn a lesson I do not retain. There is not enough oxygen in my brain for informed consent, only enough to believe I have fucked up by having asthma, by not being able to breathe in the first place. I earn my life back ten minutes of wheezing at a time, the cavern in my chest echoing the breathing patterns I force myself to maintain. When the buzzing gets too loud- when it overpowers the proof of life in the grinding of air along my esophagus- I will give in, and in doing so I know that I am weak and I have failed. It is an impossible dichotomy I have made for myself, that by surviving I am throwing away my right to be human. Which instability came first, mental or physical?

Yet I am nonchalant about the wired time bomb of my chest. I design a Spotify playlist mid-attack, trying to make my boyfriend laugh with No Air and Breathe (2 am), try to hide that I am also panicking until we can make it home. I breathe deeply, burying my face in my puppy's fluffy coat. I tempt fate roasting marshmallows one night a year, the bonfire smoke scent that lingered in my hair setting me off days later. The shower water is too hot, I can feel my airways closing, and yet I twist the knob further to the right, burning off the self-hatred and loathing for the day. I sit at peace with my wheeze for half hours at a time, an audible companion in the otherwise silence of my small apartment. I leave my inhaler in coat pockets or coffee tables, assuming I will be able to remember where it is when the inevitable strikes. I risk it, daringly, hiking trails and pushing myself harder at the gym than I should. I feel my chest tighten and my lungs constrict. I continue to run. I hear the first wheeze, I catch my shoulders rising, bad breathing technique, but my body doesn't care, I keep still and do not go for my inhaler. I will go soon, but I am fine. And in three hours I will not be fine, but I will have given in. There will be an uncomfortable heat even as my extremities cool. The skin behind my ears will burn, crying out in pain. I will not hear it. Someone will ask if I've taken a puff yet.

     I never think to remember the conscious moment I decide to give in. I don't think I like to admit when it happens. I pretend it won't. Even once I have decided that soon, in just a moment, I will get up and retrieve my survival tool, the actual adult taking care of me, the stupid red inhaler, I don't go. I wait a little longer. I pretend to myself I'm not going to get it, I'm going to be okay. It is a dangerous game to play with myself. One sided chicken, autoneurotic asphyxiation. No ropes, no belts, no markings, no signs of fall. Just a dead girl. If I miss my mark, if I push too hard, if I think I can make it when I can't, if I just want to try just a minute longer, just want to pretend I am not a broken human, and I fail, should we count it as suicide? Is an asthma attack a tragedy or my body's self-defense? Will my death certificate list my cause of death as lack of oxygen or good sense? If the simple act of being alive is dangerous, borderline deadly, then living at all is pushing my luck. Leaving the house becomes a risk. Becoming
attached. I go days, weeks, sometimes a whole month and then it is there again, a high-pitched warning signal as I gasp and gorge myself on air. It is hard for others to comprehend that my continued existence is a show of defiance, that is possible to live without the basic necessities of life. It is hard for them to understand how close to death I can be, because I cannot admit how willing I am to risk it. I stay awake to watch the sunrise, each breath grabbing deeply, tangling up with my insides and pulling, taking everything up with it that it can. My body aches for sleep and air but I have chosen death over leaving the bed for my inhaler. He is quicker to suggest the ER than I am, but he doesn't realize how often I try to skip my evening pills, try to make it through the night with my

own lungs and not drugs. I push his arm off me with faint lines of color in the sky, finally giving in, giving up. I want to be a whole person and I feel broken, left behind from snowball fights and fields of wildflowers. He's figured out how to wrap his arms around me so I feel safe but not constricted, figured out I control my inhaler because I cannot control my lungs.

I don't know if my stubbornness will kill me, if my stupidity will ever win against my need to breathe. I don't know if the condition lowers my life expectancy, if the drugs I take are quickly poisoning my liver. I know my asthma is worse than it was when I was little, now that there are cats and dogs and laughs so long I set myself off. I know I panic more now, now that I know there's a word for the feelings I have and a legitimate diagnosis for what I always thought was just something wrong with me when I was younger; some way I had screwed myself up. My medical issues are legitimate, but I no longer feel as if just because there is something wrong with me I am wrong, somehow.

Oxymoronically I have reasons to live now, things worth fighting through bursts of coughing for, even if many of those things are what makes it worse in the first place. We have come to an uneasy understanding; a truce of sorts. Years of inhaling crookedly have changed my heartbeat. I breathe, painful dragging that aches through my brittle bones, and wait for the day my air supply runs out too, the final extinction burst, and then all of the dinosaurs will be home at last.

THINK OF SOMETHING
Patrick Stebbing

"How can I make my dog a service dog?" a woman asks me. I don't know her; I've never met her before. But I came here to pick up my medications from the pharmacy, and my service dog in training caught her attention.

I know what I'm going to say; she isn't the first person to ask, and she won't be the last. "Well, it depends on what kind of service dog your dog would become. What disabilities would your dog be trained to help you with?"

"I'm sure I can think of something," she says, and I'm thinking of something, too.

I'm thinking of ten years of emotional abuse; I'm thinking of the way my grandmother laughed when I would cry, the way I felt when she said I was selfish, the way she would berate me for locking any door in the house because "What if I can't get to you? What if I need help?", the way I would hide myself in the bathroom, taking long baths to try and avoid her, only for her to open the bathroom door and take away what little personal space I tried to make for myself.

I'm thinking of pitying looks on the faces of teachers as I walked by, the way they would whisper about "that poor Stebbing girl, her mother was such a nice lady," the older kids looking at the kindergartner who lost their mom to cancer. I'm thinking of panicked teachers and a panicked principal taking a now second grader to the priest, because that second grader started sobbing in the library when the class was making Mother's Day cards.

I'm thinking of the 10 years that I spent at Catholic school, with constant reminders of the sins that I had, sins that I needed to repent for and beg forgiveness for, even when some of those sins weren't ones that I had committed, but ones that had been committed long ago by people in a book. I'm thinking of when I came out as gay and trans, how my high school counselor said I couldn't use the name I identified with, that I couldn't identify as myself because it might be harmful to me if people got upset about it. I'm thinking of how I was more hurt by being denied the right to be myself than I was of people's opinions on the matter.

I'm thinking of disembodied voices yelling at me in empty rooms, voices in my head screaming to open my skin like I open my heart and my soul for people every single day. I'm thinking of opening my skin like the voices told me to, opening myself to be read like an open book.

I'm thinking of crying into pillows at nights, trying to stay just quiet enough to keep my grandma from hearing, to keep prying eyes and ears out of my room and out of my head. I'm thinking of therapist appointments, of years of learning to say, "I am important," and years of trying to believe it.

I'm thinking of suicide attempts, of three short hospitalizations and one residential inpatient stay in the course of a year. I'm thinking of doctor after audiologist after psychiatrist after therapist after neurologist after psychologist, of medication after medication, of test after study after exam after questionnaire, of diagnosis after diagnosis after diagnosis.

I'm thinking of my first relationship, of how the word "nonbinary" rolled so smoothly off my tongue, how "trans girl" stuttered so nervously off of theirs; how we both began to say "nonbinary" so smoothly, how we fit together so seamlessly. I'm thinking of how we started to fit together a little too tightly, how I started to ask for more space, started to push them away, only to be pulled even closer, how I started to feel like I couldn't breathe.

I'm thinking of being admitted to a residential inpatient facility, of the constant screaming in the halls and the heartbeat pounding in my chest, the feeling of being both trapped and abandoned at the same time. I'm thinking of crying in hallways, panic attacks in bathrooms, a girl who comes so close but seems so nice, who follows me to my room and traps me inside, closing in on me until I can't breathe. I'm thinking of those next few weeks, being told I "just made a mistake," being called a liar, a bitch, an attention whore, a stuck-up prude.

I'm thinking of flashbacks, panic attacks, hallucinations, mood swings, self-harming, suicidal thoughts, and disordered eating. I'm thinking of being given diagnoses; of my therapist sitting me down, reading the criteria with me. *Borderline Personality Disorder*, she says. *Post-Traumatic Stress Disorder*, she says. *Major Depressive Disorder*, she says.

I'm thinking of the flood of relief, and joy, and confidence. I'm thinking of the moment when I realized this was real, this is real, *my pain is real*. I'm thinking of statistics, of the prevalence of these disorders, of the forums and groups and therapies that support people with these disorders, that support *people like me*. I'm thinking of finally feeling like I'm not the liar I was always told I was.

And as I stand by the pharmacy with my service dog in training, and this woman tells me she can "think of something," I think of how hard it's been training this dog to help me, how hard I've worked for the dog beside me to be even half as good as he'll need to be when he's fully trained, and how much harder I'm still willing to work, just to have this dog beside me, to have a dog that will help me access daily life the way most people are able to access life on their own.

I think about the journey I've made to get this far, and how much farther I still have to go; *if you don't already have something to think of that a service dog could help with, trust me, you don't want to*, I think.

THIS BODY
Kat Williams

I stretch my legs on the bed, roll a tennis ball over my shins where they're sore. I'm angry at the places higher up on my thigh, the ones that aren't hard through and through, like the knots in my calves. I'm afraid to touch the sides of my body and my stomach, where the fat is thickest, most pliable. I'm not really sure what my ab muscles feel like to touch because I'm too scared to find them with my fingers.

I could list all the parts of my body I hate. I have before, actually, which is why I know it is not art. The hated parts are joined by a simple commonality: fat. Always fat. Though I am occasionally annoyed at the smallness of my hands or the weakness of my wrists, I don't mind looking at them or acknowledging their shape. I don't fear them the way I fear the lumps of my lower back and the spot where armpit meets sports bra.

I almost wrote excess fat. But how is excess defined? It's best to be safe and have as little fat as possible.

+

In women's trade magazine terms, I am a combination of the "athletic" and "apple" body types, muscular and wide-shouldered with a tendency to hold weight in the torso. It's the archetypical German shot putter body, thought maybe shorter. It is impossible or very uncomfortable to wear readymade high waisted pants--with the waist clasped snugly, the seat billows out strangely, tent-like where the denim is meant to hug curve. I am writing this paragraph so you can see me. I am writing this so you can see me through the cultural lenses I apply to myself every day. This is as objective as I can be.

Some people have called me thin, but others have called me overweight. I absolutely benefit from thin privilege. A man I liked once told me my face looks disproportionately fatter than my body. What I'm saying is that what you are picturing in your mind may look nothing like me, depending how you define your own aesthetic terms.

I am happy with my shape in some contexts. My natural muscularity suits me to strength-based sports like powerlifting and throwing. And then the narrower structure of my thighs and hips predisposed me to faster times while marathon running. But the most powerful force behind my obsessive running was the feeling of ecstatic invincibility at the 25th mile, the brain-shattering, dopamine-fueled conviction that the extraordinary functionality of my body had rendered it perfect. I was the happiest I've ever felt about my body while crossing those finish lines.

But I was on naturally-occurring brain drugs, and that feeling left after an hour or so. I was always back to restricting and throwing up by the next day.

+

I ran three miles to the CrossFit box and when I arrived, I saw that the workout was more running. Two miles, as fast as possible. The whole time, I could see the bulges of my love handles articulated in my shadow. I ran two miles thinking only *I hate myself I have gotten so fat my boyfriend has made me fat this is unacceptable from now on I will workout every day sometimes twice a day and no more smoking weed ever it gives me munchies and I only smoke weed with my boyfriend which means he is home and can hear me throw up so no more weed I will say it's because I sleep better without it which is true but more true is that I hate my body I hate it I hate it.* I could feel my fat vibrate with every footfall.

I thought of cutting every bit of fat off with a special pair of scissors, scissors with safety blades that slide thickly through flab. In my childhood version of this daydream, the adipose slabs fell from my body cleanly, into a pile like cut hair on the barbershop floor. The after was just me, but thin--the wounds magically cauterized and erased.

In the current iteration of this fantasy, my fat is gone, but so is most of my skin. Muscle and veins, lymph nodes dangling from armpits, and the viscera of my torso glisten and steam. Eventually the body will bleed all the way out, but I don't picture this future. The present is a lifelike doll with patchwork wrist and ankle and elbow skin whose face looks like mine, but thinner.

This is the image I hold while running. This is what keeps me moving forward.

+

There are times when the many socio-cultural trappings of my hatred of my body fall away and all that's left is a frameless, blue-hot hatred. I stop thinking about my body as fat or lumpy or scarred or slumped. I forget what it looks like in the mirror. When I think, *this body*, I see only the hum of nervous energy in my fingertips and knees and spine. I watch a knot of electric impulse tease through the dark. In my mind's eye, my body is a blankness, an undefined space without light.

In the passenger's seat of my boyfriend's car, on the way to the electronics store, I misunderstand Google map's instructions and make him miss a turn. Suddenly my muscles seize and the air inside the Honda Element is not fit to breathe. I am screaming--not words or emotions, just pain. Sometimes I hate my body for keeping me alive, for letting me exist like this, through disorienting bursts of panic and hurt.

The convulsion passes through me again, and familiarity does not make the subsequent wave more bearable. I am thrashing in a way that disturbs my boyfriend. My shrieks, far away, sound hoarse, wearied. I know my boyfriend is scared before he says *You're scaring me*. He asks *What's happening*? and I am too scorched to respond. *Is the pain in your brain or in your body*?

I am still, always, wondering about the difference.

LET'S START WITH A STORY
Lena Ziegler

I was a child and there was half-a-hunk-of-ham sitting under plastic wrap on the bottom shelf of the fridge for what felt like at least three Easters, or possibly a week. Every afternoon, for whatever amount of time it stayed there, I dug my fingers into the flesh of it and pulled its pink apart hoping no one would notice the hole growing deeper in its center where my hunger had burrowed itself safe. I really believed it, that no one would notice this mass of empty space growing wider and wider, hollowing the flesh outward toward the rubbery skin that encompassed the half-a-hunk like foreskin left out too long on the kitchen counter. I should tell you, I told his story to J recently but left out the part about the half-a-hunk, and the shiny pink hole, and the foreskin (of course). I focused on the hunger. It always left me sick, like a friend who is a little too mean when they are joking, but whose company feels necessary enough that you keep putting up with the jabs and the self-consciousness. Really, though, I think he understood because if there is anything that is obvious to J (and other men who have met me) it's that there is no story I could tell about hunger that wouldn't involve making myself ill and asking for more.

Either years, or a week later, the half-a-hunk vanished from the fridge and somehow landed in the kitchen garbage, buried under spilled coffee grounds, or maybe not buried at all, but still feeling so far away and inaccessible that I had to ask my mom why she put it there. *Gone bad*, she said in more words than that. And I swear to God I mourned that fleshy mound like it was a pet that died on the floor in front of me, sprawled out and panting for love. I swear to you I really did mourn. I thought about what my afternoons would be without that beastly pink, that slimy chunk of meat I had deposited all my want into every day, for however long, when I was eight years old, waiting for someone to notice.

CONTRIBUTORS

Jason Dean Arnold's entire career has been devoted to the importance of education, from teaching in the K-12 setting to designing and teaching online courses for post-secondary. He currently serves as the director for E-Learning, Technology, and Communications at the University of Florida's College of Education. Jason has no ability to compartmentalize. As a result, his writing, visual artwork, and music (and other creative output) are all extensions of his love for learning. Website-TemporaryTranslation.com Twitter- @jasonarnold74

Robert Beveridge makes noise (xterminal.bandcamp.com) and writes poetry in Akron, OH. Recent/upcoming appearances in COG, OUT/CAST, and Up the River, among others.

Mark Brasuell is a painter, sculptor, and multimedia artist. He was born in Texas and moved to Colorado in 1987. He was tired of sandstorms and wanted to live in a place that was beautiful and green. He is a founding member of EDGE Gallery and teaches at Metro State College of Denver. He has a BFA from Texas Tech University, and a Masters Degree from The University of Denver.

Mark Brasuell was born in Texas and moved to Colorado in 1987. He is a founding member of EDGE Gallery and teaches at Metro State College of Denver. He has a BFA from Texas Tech University, and a Masters Degree from The University of Denver. MarkBrasuell.com (see cover artist statement p.53)

John M. Davis lives in Visalia, California, where he teaches at The College of the Sequoias. His work has appeared in numerous journals, including The Comstock Review, Silk Road, Reunion: The Dallas Review, Bloodroot Literary Magazine, Illya's Honey, West Trade Review, Dart. "The Mojave", a chapbook, was published by the Dallas Community Poets.

Fierce Sonia is a mixed media artist. She builds a substrate with acrylic paint and collage. A narrative is constructed by the tension between the lush layers moving to dreamy feminine mindscapes with a brighter palette. If you listen closely her work has a soundtrack, a rhythm, a pulse that will give you a magic carpet ride to a fairytale that restates your own heartbeat. She has a public studio at Torpedo Factory in Alexandria, VA.

Follow on Facebook https://www.facebook.com/fiercesonia Or @fiercesonia on Instagram

Breia Gore is an Asian-Pacific American poet living in South Carolina attending the University of South Carolina where she is pursuing a BA in English concentrated in Creative Writing and minor in film studies. Gores work has been published or is forthcoming in Lithium Magazine, Adolescent Content, Concept Literary, and Dirty Paws Press. She strives for education reforms in the arts through Teach For America and aims to create her own literary magazine to encourage youths to stay community-engaged and politically active. When she isn't stumbling over rough drafts or pointing out small animals on walks, she can be found drinking tea and organizing her pens

A self-proclaimed "creative," Lindsey Morrison Grant is an award-winning poet, screenwriter, journalist, photographer, ceramic and mixed-media artist from Portland, Oregon. She has been diagnosed with Bipolar Disorder, PTSD, ADD and various and sundry ills. As an ordained minister and State Certified Peer Support Specialist, she worked to obtain her degree in Social Work from Concordia University-Portland.

Debbie Hall is a psychologist and writer whose poetry has appeared in the San Diego Poetry Annual, A Year in Ink, Serving House Journal, Sixfold, Tuck Magazine, Poetry24, Bird's Thumb, Poetry Super Highway and other journals. She has work upcoming in an AROHO anthology. Her essays have appeared on NPR (This I Believe series), in USD Magazine, and the San Diego Union Tribune. She completed her MFA at Pacific University in Forest Grove, Oregon. Debbie is the author of the poetry collection, What Light I Have (2018, Main Street Rag Books).

Mia Herman currently serves as Outreach Director and Creative Nonfiction Editor for F(r)iction. She received an MFA in Creative Writing from Hofstra University, and her poems and essays have appeared in numerous journals, most recently the Bellevue Literary Review and Minerva Rising. When she's not writing or editing, Mia is most likely a) creating spectacular road trip playlists, b) watching obscene amounts of reality TV, or c) setting her friends up on blind dates. Follow her on Twitter @MiaMHerman.

Sean Ireland is a filmmaker/writer/producer currently residing in Santa Monica, CA. He has developed and/or participated in more than twenty feature length films. Sean is currently developing several projects, including three features, "Jailbird," "A Brewery of Eggshells," and "Girl 17." A graduate of Harvard University's ALM Masters Program in the Humanities, Sean teaches Creative Writing, English composition, World Literature, and Children's Literature at Santa Monica College and Los Angeles City College.

Anastasia Jill is a queer poet and fiction writer living in the southern United States. She is a current editor for the Smaeralit Anthology. Her work has been published or is upcoming with Poets.org, Lunch Ticket, FIVE:2:ONE, Ambit Magazine, apt, Into the Void Magazine, 2River, Requited Journal, and more.

Anna Kaye-Rogers' previous work has been published in Illinois Valley Community College River Currents, The Feminine Collective, Eastern Iowa Review, Zoetic Press Non-Binary Review, Cosmonauts Avenue, Pen 2 Paper, and Zimbell House Publishing. She received the Editor's Choice Award in Non-Fiction in Northern Illinois University Towers 2017. Upcoming work will be featured in Coffin Bell Journal and IO Literary Journal. Studies English, Creative Writing, and Professional Communications at Northern Illinois University.

Simone Liggins earned her MFA in Writing at the Jack Kerouac School of Disembodied Poetics of Naropa University. The foundation for her love of writing and literature was paved at an early age and blossomed during her teenage years through the kind of tortured freedom that only the ostracism of high school can grant a person. Her various influences include but are not limited to: Sylvia Plath, Kurt Vonnegut, Dorothy Parker, Audre Lorde, Lenore Kandel, Laurell K. Hamilton, Octavia Butler, The Beatles, Lady Gaga, Fiona Apple, and Jimi Hendrix. Her work has appeared in/on Raven Chronicles, Outsider Poetry, Boulder Weekly, Petrichor Magazine, and BEATS poetry.

ari lips is a black girl from the south who's into cold weather and dope lines. she is an active member of Black Lives Matter 5280, and a founding member of Denver Action Medic Network currently paying the bills working in behavioral health. this dedication to social justice and affinity for the advocacy of marginalized people informs much of her work. as a self-ascribed poet/activist she is best known for her uncanny ability to get lost and come back to herself ad nauseum, hence the moniker 'the prodigal negress'.

Jonathan May grew up in Zimbabwe as the child of missionaries. He lives and teaches in Memphis, TN, where he served as the inaugural Artist in Residence at the Memphis Brooks Museum of Art. In addition, May has taught writing as therapy for people with eating disorders. He serves as Editor-in-Chief of antinarrative journal. Read more at https://memphisjon.wordpress.com/

Jacob Newman is a sophomore at the University of Colorado. Artist statement: "I am a cartoonist, and a lot of my work deals with the changing nature of our social lives, which of course is disproportionately impacted by the way that we use our phones. I believe that in a lot of the art that we consume today, we have not advanced our depictions of phone use with the pace that our usage has changed. It is therefore a goal of mine to accurately depict cellphone addiction and its tangible consequences on our lives. The image that I am sending you is a play on the famous "Rainy Day In Paris". I have depicted a city scene where people are walking almost mechanically, as they did in the original. However, in my scene, people are encapsulated by their phones. The original picture was meant to comment on the mechanized realities of city life at the time, and I have created my own take on this image in a more modern context by depicting a mechanized city life as we experience it today, tied to our phones and unable to be present in our world."

Rachele Salvini. Although she is based in Oklahoma, where she is doing her PhD in English and Creative Writing, she is an Italian student writing in English. She did her MA in London, UK. Her work in English has been published on Takahe Magazine, Erotic Review, Crack the Spine Magazine, Aerogramme Writers' Studio and others. This short story was published on The Machinery India in 2017.

Gerard Sarnat won the Poetry in the Arts First Place Award plus the Dorfman Prize, has been nominated for Pushcarts and authored four collections: HOMELESS CHRONICLES (2010), Disputes (2012), 17s (2014) and Melting The Ice King (2016) which included work published by Oberlin, Brown, Columbia, Johns Hopkins and in Gargoyle, Margie, Main Street Rag, MiPOesias, New Delta Review, Brooklyn Review, Los Angeles Review of Books, Voices Israel, Tishman Review, Suisun Valley Review, Burningwood Review, Fiction Southeast, Junto, Tiferet plus featured in New Verse News, Eretz, Avocet, LEVELER, tNY, StepAway, Bywords, Floor Plan, Good-Man-Project, Anti-Heroin-Chic, Poetry Circle, Fiction Southeast and Tipton Review. "Amber Of

Memory" was the single poem chosen for my 50th college reunion symposium on Bob Dylan. Mount Analogue selected Sarnat's sequence, KADDISH FOR THE COUNTRY, for pamphlet distribution on Inauguration Day 2017 as part of the Washington DC and nationwide Women's Marches. For Huffington Post/other reviews, readings, publications, interviews; visit his site. Harvard/Stanford educated, Gerry's worked in jails, built/staffed clinics for the marginalized, been a CEO and Stanford Med professor. Married for a half century, Gerry has three kids and four grandkids so far.   www.GerardSarnat.com

Evan James Sheldon's work has appeared in Pithead Chapel, Pif, CHEAP POP, Spelk, Levee, Roanoke Review, and Ghost City Review, among others. He is a junior editor and outreach assistant for F(r)iction.

Patrick Stebbing is a college student studying psychology and American Sign Language (ASL). As a mentally ill person, a nonbinary and queer person, a biracial person, and a person with "invisible disabilities," They hope to bring not just awareness, but acceptance to minority communities of all kinds.

Dustin Stephens is a student studying Human Development, with minors in Education and Music, at the University of California, Davis. There, his passion for poetry, arts, and for caring deeply for others has grown greatly. He hopes to one day be an educator and poet.

Dennis James Sweeney's writing has appeared in The Collagist, Crazyhorse, Five Points, Indiana Review, and Passages North, among others. He is the Small Press Editor of Entropy, an Assistant Editor of Denver Quarterly, the recipient of an MFA from Oregon State University, and a recent Fulbright fellow in Malta. Originally from Cincinnati, he lives in Colorado, where he is a PhD student in Creative Writing at the University of Denver.

Kat Williams is a queer writer and animal obsessive living in Austin, TX. Their work can be read in Autostraddle and Cutbank's All Accounts and Mixture.

Lena Ziegler is the editor and co-founder of the literary journal The Hunger. She holds an MFA in Creative Writing from Western Kentucky University, and is pursuing her PhD in Rhetoric and Writing at Bowling Green State University. She has been a finalist in GoldLine Press's Non-fiction Chapbook contest. Her work has appeared or is forthcoming in

Yes, Poetry, The Seventh Wave, Dream Pop Press, Gambling the Aisle, Red Earth Review, Miracle Monocle, Breathe Free Press, Fredericksburg Literary and Arts Review, and others.

COVER ARTIST STATEMENT

Mark Brasuell
"Süßigkeiten" (German for "candy")

I use energy, emotion, and a physicality in creating my artwork. I usually start out with a vague idea about the emotional impact I want the piece to have, but I rarely have any thought-out plan of what the finished piece will look like. I let my intuition, body movement, and emotional state guide the piece out of my mind and onto the canvas or drawing surface. I reserve all judgment until the final stages of the piece.

I have often said that I hate painting. I mean that sometimes the process can be excruciating for me, because I am not satisfied with what the painting looks like prior to being finished. However, the last 10 or 15 minutes of the painting is the best part. In a way it is exactly like a drug. I get euphoric and excited about how it turns out. I think to myself, "That is what I was thinking". Really, without thinking at all.

For the last several years I have focused on what I call conceptual abstraction. It is based on color, action, and some personal and emotional "ideas" There is usually a background and foreground, vibrant and moody colors, and an occasional ghostly image or two. I want people to make up their own minds about exactly what these images are, but I try to point the viewer in a particular direction. I want people to enjoy my artwork and to see something new in the paintings every time they view them.

www.MarkBrasuell.com

Buddy publishes writing of any style and on any topic, but we are a safe space for writing about any mental health issue, including a range of psych-social-biological concerns. We're also building on some community involvement, such as our book drive for mental health clientele.

See our site for more info.

Contact us via email to donate books, or to receive books for your patients.

www.BuddyLitZine.com
info@BuddyLitZine.com
Facebook.com/BuddyLitZine
Twitter.com/BuddyLitZine
BuddyLitZine.submittable.com/submit
#BuddyKeepWriting